I0494001

Disclaimer

Summary

Planning to setup your own business? Indeed, becoming an entrepreneur comes with its set of prerequisites. First and foremost, you become your boss and people look up to you for advice and instructions. However, there are risks associated with owning your business that you must not ignore.

If you are reading this book, congratulations! You have put your hands on the right set of information, which will guide you systematically to set up your own business and become an entrepreneur.

This book will cover:

1. Basic steps to reach out and get involved in setting up your own business
2. Detail on the 5-stages of entrepreneurial development
3. A checklist of characteristic properties to recognize the entrepreneur within you
4. A systematic entrepreneurship plan
5. Learning about different businesses to enter the right market for your first time experience

When I left the corporate world to pursue my entrepreneurial dreams, I quickly learned that one needed to put as much (if not more) effort into creating a successful business---there are many great advantages to being your own boss, but there are also a lot more challenges.

If you believe you have what it takes to become a successful entrepreneur, use the information available in this book and get started now.

Contents

Introduction – Reaching out and Getting Involved

Preparing yourself to establish your own business and become an entrepreneur may appear as a formidable task. You may believe that learning specific skills such as business practices and finance is crucial for marketing and manufacturing products.

While these topics are indeed important, they are not difficult. If you have made up your mind and are really interested, it is actually easy to learn these subjects and do great in no time.

In addition to these subjects, what will really make a difference is your approach and the strategy that you are using for your business.

To start with, think of it this way: business is about people and the transactions. Thus, in addition to strategies and approach, it is also important that you build a foundation of mutual relationship and trust with the people you are dealing with.

Acquiring Knowledge Base to Establish Your Own Business

You need to be creative in order to put up a good strategy. The keys to creativity are your problem-solving skills and your knowledge base. People who started as beginners and did great over time tend to have 'street smart strategies'. This is based on unusual ways to solving problems and seeing things.

The problems of business are different from technical problems; meaning, business problems tend to have more boundary conditions, which are often changing, unpredictable and poorly defined.

Therefore, you have to focus on changing your strategies over time and remain sensitive to the environment as new information enters the market.

Building Problem Solving Skills

Physical science is all about dealing with concrete answers and defined principles. However, a practical business is all about uncertainty and risks. It is more like chess. You need to understand complex situations and plan moves beforehand. What could really save you here is making sound decisions, and sharpening your skills of understanding the complexity of a situation.

The best way to improve these skills is by developing a habit of always thinking one step ahead to come up with several outcomes for a single scenario.

Focusing on the Current Market and Environment

In order to start a successful business, you must develop sensitivity towards the environment and business trends. In short, you need to focus on the market and the current happenings before deciding to invest in any product or project.

A little economics will help you here. Focus on the demand and supply before you set out to manufacture and market your products. For instance, if you are planning to introduce any test-based instrument, you must look at the market for the demand of the instrument in order to proceed. If the prices have been falling drastically together with the demand of the product, the product is already considered a fail.

In short, a sense of environment can definitely help you fine-tune your business strategies.

Bottom Line

Before you set out to understand other, first understand yourself. If you want to become an entrepreneur and start your own business, it is very important that you know how to deal with difficult situations and difficult people.

Thus, getting involved and reaching out to helping people is the ideal way to prepare yourself to become your own boss. It is give to get!

Preparing Yourself to Become an Entrepreneur – The 5-Stages of Entrepreneurial Development

So who's an entrepreneur? What does 'becoming your own boss' really mean?

Well, it is important to understand that entrepreneurship brings with it a long list of responsibilities. An entrepreneur is a businessperson, who not only establishes and organizes ventures, but also often takes risks during the process.

Not all businesspersons are real entrepreneurs. Different levels of entrepreneurial drive and intensity depend upon the level of independence and competence one demonstrates, the degree of innovation and leadership they exhibit, the level of responsibility they shoulder, and the intensity of how creative they can be in executing and envisioning their entrepreneurship plan.

The journey of a successful entrepreneurial development starts with basic employment. It is based on the understanding that good and hardworking employees often evolve to become great entrepreneurs. However, in order to be successful, you must seek out a role and adopt a perspective much more than that of an employee.

The following are the 5 stages of entrepreneurial development, crucial for successful entrepreneurship journey.

Stage 1 – The Right Mindset for Self-Employment

What is the emotional driving force that works for a successful entrepreneur or a self-employed person? To your surprise, it is not the security. In fact, it is a desire to obtain greater control over his or her career, life, and destiny.

Giving away that control to an individual (their boss) every day for 8-9 consecutive hours does not bring them any happiness. In fact, it leads to a belief that the job can be done just as well without an employer over their head – and perhaps, even without other employees.

In short, they require more autonomy and wish to do things their own way. Sadly, most of the fundamental objectives that a person sets to become an entrepreneur with the mindset of self-employment are traps or pitfalls. Since the mindset is about going alone, they usually do it at their own risk. Since they cut themselves from any outside help or assistance, they deprive themselves from valuable experience, feedback, intelligence, and talent that others could have offered. However, this allows them to enjoy freedom they never did during employment.

When I decided to quit my corporate job to pursue my entrepreneurial endeavors, it was one of the most terrifying and exciting moments of my life. I wanted to take control of my life and stop being the lackey for horrible bosses. It was the best decision I made because I'm a much happier person. Now I am a full-time entrepreneur achieving my dreams.

Most entrepreneurs hold on to a very strong, do-it-yourself mindset, and are only successful in creating self-employment for themselves, i.e. only a job and not a profitable company or a new career. And since they are the only performer for their business, the job becomes extremely consuming. They never enjoy a day off from work, they have piled up work that even needs attention at home, and they are forced to operate overtime for which they are not financially compensated.

Thus, the mindset of being 'self-employed' plays a significant role on how you will succeed in a business. While freedom is important, working as a sole-operator of the business is not the right approach. One of the most common mistakes people make when they plan to become self-employed entrepreneurs is that they replicate similar jobs they have been doing, in the same industry and in the same area of expertise and experience, selling or marketing a service or product they are familiar with.

While it may sound a little counterintuitive to operate in a completely unfamiliar territory and in a different direction, that trajectory will put you in a position of being open-minded towards learning new things, and relying on experts for assistance. These are the successful ingredients to prepare a successful entrepreneurial recipe, because these ingredients will force you to evaluate your own business system from a completely new and innovative perspective.

If you understand this fact, you are ready to move to the next level of entrepreneurship.

Stage 2 – Learning the Managerial Perspective

Employees responsible for managerial outlook are usually in a better position to be successful as entrepreneurs, except for a few misconceptions that could result in big problems.

A majority of managers believe that hiring more employees is the only solution to make a business work. What they don't realize is that hiring a larger workforce to tackle the problem will only worsen the situation. A larger hierarchy can make it difficult for the team to reach to the underlying root cause of the lack of profitability.

Another common misconception among managers is that the only way to be successful is through growth – and growth here does not address the profit growth but the growth of the overall structure of the enterprise. Again, bigger does not necessarily mean it will be better, until and unless the fundamentals are efficient and sound.

Growing bigger in order to tackle business problems will only lead to a business with a larger workforce than required and problems will become much more magnified, expanded, and expensive to take care of. For these few reasons, most new entrepreneurs with a 'managerial mindset' go into bankruptcy.

Another common misstep of this managerial attitude is that entrepreneurs behave like a boss, even if that means giving up the potential or talent of employees. To lead and hold the charge requires no aptitude or great skill, but leadership – to know how to train and inspire the workforce and to rise to greater height – now that's a great feat. Managers who accept entrepreneurship with leadership in mind succeed because they accept the responsibility and challenge of ensuring that the workforce performs at their highest potential so that the business can flourish.

Thus, managers who really know how to lead can make the most out their employees. This helps them lead to the next level and become not only the boss, but also an inspiration and leader for the workforce. This takes them one step closer to the real concept of entrepreneurship.

Stage 3 – The Leadership Attitude

The leadership attitude is the key to success while establishing your new business as an entrepreneur. The entrepreneur who gains the level of a leader/owner, experiences amazing benefits by realizing that employees play a significant role in the success of a business, and by stepping aside, they can allow the business to operate as a profit center without relying on the constant contribution and participation of the owner.

This way, owners are able to establish an organization, which is not only self-sustaining, but also self-sufficient. This allows the new entrepreneurs to create more free time, personal freedom, and wealth.

Rather than standing alone as the sole operator of the business, the quality of leadership allows the owner to pass the torch of expertise and responsibility to others who have the better skills and expertise to perform the job. The leader/owner is able to focus better on net profits. While the business operations are running smoothly, the owner is able to concentrate on the profitability while allowing others to take care of the daily operational details.

Stage 4 – The Entrepreneurial Investor

For an entrepreneur who has succeeded in establishing a business generating regular profits, it becomes easier to proceed and accept more challenges. This calls for money management, so that the business can make more money.

Investing to gain maximum returns involves the leverage of assets, and an entrepreneurial investor knows how to exploit the success of one business in order to establish another one based on the same system or model.

By investing in a separate healthy business or franchising a successful venture, the investor can expand his or her career by not only selling the basic services and products, but also selling the overall businesses. However, the goal remains the same – to turn as big of a profit as possible.

Therefore, instead of remaining at the helm of the businesses, the investor will invest in them, ensuring they are of valuable equity or attractive potential and allure, and later will sell them to other entrepreneurs. In short, the focus is diverted from business operations to finding, investing (perhaps renovating) businesses to re-sell, exactly like a real estate investor finds homes, refurbishes them, and sells them for the sake of profit.

Unfortunately, this does not come without pitfalls. The biggest challenge here is to avoid falling back to your initial role of operating a business as a manager or administrator, and to face this situation with a solution. The investor becomes more of a silent partner or a director who shares in the profits while taking complete advantage of not sharing the responsibility or funding or managing of the business.

All of this is only possible when an entrepreneur does not only focus on establishing a business, but has an excellent system in hand to keep it going. At this point, the entrepreneurial investor has risen to the level of comprehensive and broad strategies that work across all types of economic cycles, products, and services.

All in all, working hard is replaced by working smart, and entrepreneurs gain abundant rewards – both personal and financial.

Stage 5 – The True Leader/Entrepreneur

By evolving throughout the entrepreneurial development stages, and learning at every step, you reach the highest level of accomplishment. At this point, you can easily achieve your ultimate goal and realize that your dreams are making their way to you.

The true leader/entrepreneur enjoys a paradigm shift that includes a process comprised of four steps of altered thinking:

Idealization – Create gigantic imaginative, all-encompassing dreams to establish your very own ideal world.

Verbalization – Think of your dream or goal and begin putting words to it as if you were already achieving it. Speak of it in front of others as if everything is real and don't hesitate in having a personal dialogue to make it a reality.

Visualization – Use the power of visualization, and picture the ideal world as your reality. Start clarifying your vision on a regular basis, filling in more details to it every time.

Materialization – Since you have the intention and effort of believing and designing in the dream and the ideal, things will eventually start falling into place and occur in an automatic and natural way. Your small idea takes the shape of reality, tangible facts materialize in the world and creates and influences others while building new opportunities, which eventually give rise to more dreams.

A true entrepreneur can be defined as a dreamer, whose dreams take the shape of reality, and soon he becomes a successful businessperson, earning a huge income. Everything eventually has a snowball effect, and money made is put to use to make more money. True entrepreneurs can add to their wealth by taking possession of more profit centers, more paper assets, and eventually more entrepreneurial powers.

One Dozen Characteristic Checks Essential for Entrepreneurs

By evaluating the 5 stages of entrepreneurial development, we are not in a better position to understand the fundamentals that differentiates between extraordinary entrepreneurs from ordinary ones. This allows us to outline the traits and qualities that are a must-have for all entrepreneurs to be successful.

Naturally, a number of individual entrepreneurs possess qualities and traits that are very unique and not common amongst other entrepreneurs. Almost all of them are believed to share kindred spirit, a certain type of outlook and constitution, and a special willingness and drive.

Here are a dozen characteristics that can be found with all successful entrepreneurs. Compare yourself with the checklist below and see if you fall short of what it takes to be a successful entrepreneur.

Level of Confidence

The truth is: confidence is a hallmark of the entrepreneurship. While many of us are born with this trait, not all of us are good in this department. However, this does not mean we cannot develop the required level of confidence. A number of confident men and women gain their sense of faith and self-esteem in their ability to accept challenge through actions. Even if there is a lack of confidence, gaining belief and strength by picturing the results can get them respect and praise from others.

The Sense of Being the Boss

If you are the boss, you are the one responsible too! It is important that entrepreneurs feel a sense of ownership and are responsible towards it. Considering themselves responsible for getting things done with attention and care is what others expect from them.

When performing in a team, even others' problems should be considered like your own, and you should put your best foot forward in finding a solution. The sense of ownership boosts your capabilities of solving problems and leaving them in much better shape than they were before you encountered them.

Make sure you have it in you to do what it takes to lead a business, control a situation, and take risks.

Communication Skills

Undoubtedly, the human element is the most significant part of any business as recognized by the entrepreneurs. Human resource – whether they are your employees, customers, or strategic partners – is the main source that can make or break your business. Therefore, in order to make the most of your human resources, remember that communication is the key to establish successful relationships.

As an entrepreneur, you must work to improve your communication skills, so that you are able to use your resources in the best possible manner for the advantage of your business. You must hone your communication skills, whether they are spoken, written, or non-verbal messages given through body language.

Don't forget to use all the available resources and tools to your advantage and support your communication skills. These resources and tools include public speaking classes or foreign language classes, telecom and computer technology, neurolinguistic programming or search engine optimization --- all these relate to marketing and sales. You can even opt for specialized writing skills that are required for business proposals, grants, policy manuals, or mission statements.

In addition to this, an entrepreneur is expected to listen what others have to say, because the best communication skills can only be developed if you are a good listener.

Passion for Learning

Good entrepreneurs are usually 'autodidactic' learners. This means, much of what you know and have learned is not a result of your academic learning but your experiences. This includes asking questions, seeking out information, and putting an effort for personal research and reading.

Passionate entrepreneurs are also quick learners, especially when it comes to learning from their own mistakes. This reduces the level of business risk naturally. They are also less prone to repeat their mistakes due to ego, arrogance, or blindness towards their own errors, shortcomings, and faults.

Another way they learn with time is by teaching. They impart experience, train and lead their employees and other fellow entrepreneurs, and eventually learn more than they know and learn things differently from how they knew it.

If you want to be a great entrepreneur, make sure you have the capabilities of entertaining the perspectives and views of other people, and learn with the experience of others. This way you will be able to enrich yourself with continuous learning and knowledge, which you can share with your employees to take your business to the next level.

Team Play

A competent entrepreneur or leader is expected to be a great team player as well. Those entrepreneurs, who step into the business for themselves and fail to utilize their team, usually wind up without any work done.

It is important to understand and realize that the goal behind setting up your own venture is bigger than you think. The responsibility can be too heavy for you to shoulder, and thus, your attempt to be successfully self-employed can fail without team play.

New ventures come with greater financial and personal risk. Therefore, it is important to utilize your team players, as they are skilled to succeed by utilizing the physics of dynamic relationships and interpersonal synergy.

Dedication

Successful entrepreneurs dedicate themselves to accomplish their visions, plans, and dreams. Focus and dedication are extremely essential factors to run a new business successfully. One of the biggest reasons that most companies fail at inception is because the entrepreneurs give up dedication and lose focus. Keep your goal in mind, clarify the objective of your business, fine-tune the brand, and narrow the probabilities of making mistakes.

Regardless of the level of effort required to achieve your goal, an entrepreneur is successful if he or she is able to bring a single-minded dedication towards the goal.

An entrepreneur, by being committed to a positive outcome and willing and ready to do the needful, can be successful.

System-Oriented

Just like mathematics, if you have a good system formula in place, you are surely going to achieve great results – with less exertion of resources or energy. Entrepreneurs should first rely on their system before they are dependent on their team, and seek for a system-based solution before looking for solutions that are human based.

Thus, spend time and come up with a system plan that works, so even if you fall short on human resources at any point, your business will not be threatened.

Optimistic Approach

A positive approach is crucial for successful entrepreneurs. Being optimistic helps them learn to view a setback as a bargain priced lesson of a valuable business firsthand. Past disappointments, failures, and shortcomings are left behind so that their effects do not obstruct or haunt the present or the future. And when this helps the business to prosper, it further fuels the positive mindset and optimism of an entrepreneur, which further increases hopefulness and greater accomplishments.

Training

Once you have decided to enter the business and have analyzed your weaknesses and strengths, it is time to focus on training. You might identify deficiencies as you proceed with your business operations, and you may feel like there is a need for training. Such training could be:

1. Changing attitude positively and developing skills –
    Business Management and Entrepreneurship Training
    skills
2. Developing work/technical skills for proposed
    project/product

Gregarious

Don't forget, business is all about people and thus,
entrepreneurs are successful when they are socially outgoing.
It makes them excited and happy about sharing products,
services, and ideas, and the excitement and happiness is
contagious to their friends, clients, employees, and contacts
both beyond and within the business sphere.

However, men and women who put effort as entrepreneurs
also enjoy the unique experience of running a successful
business. Business psychologists, career counselors, and
human resource experts, all agree that those who do jobs that
they love or are interested in, enjoy broader levels of
satisfaction.

Set an Example as a Leader

As mentioned earlier, entrepreneurs should set themselves as
leaders. Not only should they lead themselves through self-
motivation, but should also use that to motivate their team.
Only leaders know the importance of self-motivation and
teamwork, and the imperativeness of appreciating them,
rewarding them, and supporting them accordingly.

Only true leaders do not become indispensable. They make
sure things remain intact, even in their absence, and the team
performs regardless of any pressure and only out of self-
motivation.

Not Afraid of Success or Risk

A leader or successful entrepreneur should never be afraid of success or risks. In fact, most of the people who are successful today took chances and great risks once. Make sure you prioritize things as you approach your business success.

Believe it or not, frustration, fear of failure, drudgery, dissatisfaction, and boredom can never outweigh the happiness of success, if you prioritize things the right way.

Setting-Up the Entrepreneurship Plan

If you want to establish and run your own business, here we will discuss the setup plan to help you do so. Being an entrepreneur is a high-rewarding, high-risk position. While there are many stressful situations, you will also experience a great sense and reward of accomplishment. Most importantly, it is not as difficult as it may seem – as long as you hold on to patience, diligence, and of course, a good system, and entrepreneurial plan. You will be your own boss in no time!

Come Up With a Great Idea

According to experts, the inception of most businesses is based on one great idea – whether it is about providing a product in the market, or a service people require, or a combination of both. Don't forget that the idea has very little significance, it is what you do with it that matters!

1. If you have a great idea in mind, evaluate it realistically. Think about the cost, marketing, manufacturing time, demand, price, and popularity.
2. Don't just stick to one idea. Be open to different options and ideas always. If you consider it necessary, conduct a market research beforehand and see if you really have a market for a product or service you have in mind.
3. If you are completely open to ideas for your business and have nothing in mind yet, a good start is to check out your target market first. Prepare a list of the type of potential customers you will have, their buying habits, and the type of things they like. Next, narrow this list,

25

keeping the following three things in mind and comparing it with the product or service you have in your mind: popularity, manufacturing time and cost. Now brainstorm again and come up with the most realistic and easiest idea you can offer.

Jot Down Your Business Plan

Do you have a business plan in your hand? If not, it's time to put it up together. Include descriptions and details, and keep your planning realistic throughout. Invest time in evaluating each and every section of your product or service in detail.

The sections of a successful business plan often include:

1. The description of your product: Develop a product to run your business. Think about it: How will you design it? What is the list of materials or human resources you require to manufacture it? How will you make your product interesting and eye-catching?
2. Market analysis of your product: Where does the market for your product exist? What are the main areas they shop? What's the location of your target market? How much are they willing to pay?
3. Level of Competition: Identify your competitors – Who are your competitors? What are their strengths and weaknesses? What price are they charging? How can you beat them?
4. Marketing: How will you introduce your product in the market? What marketing strategies will you use to spread the word about your products? What type of image will earn you buyers? What are your advertising medium options? What tagline to use? What sort of packaging will be the most eye-catching?

5. Sales: Where are you planning to introduce and sell your products? How can you persuade your customers to buy your product? What's the right time to sell your product? Also, define and follow your estimated sales forecast.
6. Product Manufacturing: How to design and create your product? The material and workforce (skills) required to make your product. Define details step by step. When and where are you planning to make your product? What is your cost of goods sold?
7. Finance: How much capital do you require to get your business started? How much gross profit will you make?

Actually, a business is totally a work of fiction without any experience. If you are completely inexperienced, or the market is unknown and new, a business plan could be a total waste. Therefore, instead of planning from the scratch for up to a year's forecast, just focus on introducing the product and making your first sale.

Hire a skilled and experienced team to help you with it. Set your goal to make at least one sale or one customer happy, and experience the cycle of making products and selling products. Once you are able to do so, you will be in a better position to understand what a business really is, what business problems are, and how you can rely on extensive planning to find a solution.

You require both the bank and investors to help you set up a business plan. To make sure you do not fail to put up the best impression, present your business in the standard business plan format.

The following are two formats – simple and detailed – to help you understand the standard formats. Even the most renowned and well-established businesses today function on these standard formats. Only when you have built your business plan, you can learn to organize it.

Following the Simple Outline

Executive Summary

While we are mentioning this first, do it last. Don't forget to put up an executive summary – just a page or two long – that highlights all the important points related to your business. It also holds great importance because it is the doorway for your business plan. As your target reader goes through your executive summary, he or she will make the final decision. Your executive summary can be the determining factor whether they should support your business plan or reject it.

Company Summary

To come up with a complete business plan, a company summary is essential. This part covers you and your business. It summarizes your business vision and what you are planning to provide to your market. However, it should also inform the target reader about the nuts and bolts of your business: details like when your company was founded, history, details about owner/owners, your position in the company, how and where do you fulfill the operations, about your business' growth trajectory and even some details about your recent sales.

Services and Products

A business plan is incomplete if you do not describe your business objective – the products and services you sell. The best way to put up this information is to keep it according to customer benefits and customer requirement. Keeping that perspective in mind, define your product offerings, instead of focusing on service costs that falls on your part. Mostly, such plans include proper charts and tables that give more insights, such as a detailed price list or a bill of materials.

A Summary on Market Analysis

Explain your business activity and the type of business you are dealing in. You need to learn about your market and the changing trends. You also need to focus on the needs of your customers, their demand, ways to reach them and to deliver them your products efficiently. Also, learn about your competitors and develop tactics to stand strong against them. You need to think of all the reasons you find yourself very suitable for this market.

Summary for Strategy and Implementation

First of all, you need to describe your strategic position – What distinguishes you from your competitors and what measures are you taking for your market. In the next part, you must cover how you plan to develop or keep up with loyal customer base. Here, you need to be really specific. Make sure you mention budgets and dates when talking about management responsibilities.

Management Summary

Discuss in detail about your business organization. Also, don't forget to mention the key members of your organization management team. Include summaries about the experience and backgrounds of your managers – these could be like short resumes – and talk about their role within the company.

Financial Plan

You are expected to include the following in this section:

1. Cash flow tables
2. Profit and loss
3. Descriptions of your sales forecasts
4. Balance sheet
5. Break-even analysis
6. Business ratios

Following a Detailed Outline

Here is a detailed business plan outline to further help you understand and implement the standard format while setting up your business.

Executive Summary

1. Mission
2. Objectives
3. Keys to success

Company Summary

1. Company start-up plan (if new) or history (if ongoing)
2. Company ownership
3. Company facilities and locations

Services and Products

1. Competitive comparison
2. Service and product description
3. Sales literature
4. Technology
5. Fulfillment and sourcing
6. Future services and products

Market Analysis Summary

1. Segment strategy for target market
2. Market segmentation
3. Requirements of the market
4. Market growth
5. Changing market trends
6. Analysis of the industry

7. Participants of the industry
8. Distribution patterns
9. Main competitors
10. Buying patterns and competition
11. Distribution patterns

Summary of Strategy and Implementation

1. Value propositions
2. Strategy pyramids
3. Marketing strategy
4. Competitive edge
5. Pricing strategy
6. Positioning statements
7. Distribution patterns
8. Promotion strategy
9. Marketing programs
10. Sales forecasts
11. Sales strategies
12. Milestones
13. Strategic alliances

Management Summary

1. Management team
2. Organizational structure
3. Personnel plan
4. Management team gaps

Financial Plan

1. Financial indicators
2. Important financial assumptions
3. Profit and loss projected
4. Break-even analysis
5. Cash flow projected

6. Balance sheet projected
7. Long-term plan
8. Business financial ratios

Get Investors

Getting investors for your new business, or especially as a new entrepreneur, can be challenging. If you do not have enough capital to initiate your own setup, you will need to get investors. If you have a successful and reality-based idea in your hand, it's time to pitch it to your potential investors to get the finances to start your business.

If you have a good, convincing idea, they will be interested to invest their money in your business (either for a share or at an interest).

1. Make sure you are ready with your proposal. Prepare a detailed yet informative and interesting PowerPoint Presentation (or something similar), explaining your business idea and defining your unique product, disclosing all the unique qualities it has. Don't forget to add each section of your business (covered above) in your business plan presentation for your investors for maximum details.

2. Disclose your estimated gross profit to your investors as well as offer them a desired percentage of share they will earn as a result of profit you earn in your business. Many venture capitalists (VCs) are not established to make you rich or successful. You will actually be successful when you will be earning at least $80,000 a year, doing something you always wanted to do.

3. Focusing only on a small number of customers and starting business on a small scale with a small capital

at first is a high-probability way to reach there. A venture capitalist will not let you reach that level of success, because their main aim is to make billions by rolling the dice on other low-scale, potentially huge-returning businesses. There's a price you pay to allow a VC to intervene in your business – and the price is the control over your dreams. If you can setup and run your business on your own, without huge capital or require investors, it will be the most ideal route for you and in your best interest.

Product Marketing, Distribution and Selling

One of the biggest challenges faced by entrepreneurs and small businesses today is to market effectively. However, a number of marketing strategies can be used to make your product or service a big hit on the first go. When planning the marketing, distribution and selling plan, don't forget that small businesses may also face the hurdle of a limited budget.

However, a good marketing strategy, distribution, and selling plan is an essential tool for the success of any business. You need to introduce your products or services to the people so that they know your brand as well as the products and services you offer.

1. Make an online presence. The World Wide Web has become the largest market and international platform for all entrepreneurs to introduce and market their products and services. Make sure you make the most out of this opportunity. Establish your very own website, which can deliver results. A nicely designed, informative, and interesting website that is easy to navigate can be your most powerful took in marketing your business. Other than your business website, your

social media presence is another great way to gain more and more customers for your business. Last but not least, do not underestimate the importance of running a blog for your business. Share news about your products, interesting deals and unique services, and catch more eyes than ever.

2. Build your email list. Learn about the benefits of email marketing if you are not already aware of it. Build your email list right from the beginning and make blogging your top priority.

3. Learn to convert your website traffic into leads. The website traffic you earn becomes almost useless if you fail to convert them into customers for your business. There are many ways to do it. For example:
   a. Use an effective 'call to action' on your website.
   b. Use an effective 'call to action' in all other marketing material.
   c. Display the 'call to action' prominently on your website and other online marketing material resources.

4. Offer deals and discounts to catch the eye of your customers at the first glance. Offering deals and discounts is a great way to introduce your products or services, reward customers and market your business. Don't forget to promote your offers on your website, social media profiles, blog posts, and articles. This will allow you to enjoy extra coverage for your business.

5. Word of mouth marketing still works wonders! Providing excellent quality products and services can be convincing enough for your customers to market your products and services on your behalf. So give them a reason to share their good experience with your products and services with their social circle and see your customers growing in no time.

6. As far as selling your products is concerned, first of all, make sure you are as enthusiastic about selling your product as you expect your customers to be about buying it. When you love what you do, customers trust your business more. Tell your potential customers about the product as much as possible. The more knowledgeable they are about the product, the more they will be interested to purchase. Sell where you are able to connect with the buyer and where they are most interested in buying. For instance, if the market for your products and services is more physically important, a showroom could be the right place to sell your products. However, if you are getting a great response online, you can start off from selling online first before you decide to establish a proper setup for your business.

Marketing Made Efficient – The significance of Social Media to Market Your Business

Small and new businesses need more marketing to establish themselves in the market. However, cost can become an obstacle for businesses to market frequently and efficiently. But if you are planning to move your marketing efforts online, you can save a lot of money and time, and can target a larger market at the same time.

The following are some interesting and effective online marketing methods that any small business can implement for success.

Use Weblogs/Blogs to Your Benefit

You don't have to be a professional blogger to gain benefits from blogging online. Blogging comes in various formats and the key is to connect with your customers in the most comfortable way.

1. Try using traditional penned blogs.
2. Try podcasting, which requires you to record audio and share with your customers.
3. You can even try micro-blogging on Twitter and use minimal words to engage prospects and hold a simple conversation.

Believe it or not, blogging is an essential component of social media marketing since it enables businesses to use active online/social platforms to market their business and provide information using relevant, fresh content.

Establish an Online Network for Your Business

So we are talking about the social media platforms here. But why has social media become such a critical platform for business online marketing?

Because:

1. Social networks are one of the most addictive and popular web mediums to reach online consumers.
2. Social media platforms allow business professionals and consumers to network among other professionals, acquaintances, friends, family, and strangers all in one place.
3. Social network are a cost free option that enable businesses to update their online consumers about new products or improvement in their service line.
4. Some of the most popular and commonly used social media websites have captured the highest number of consumers all around the world. This gives a better opportunity to businesses to target larger markets in a single go. The most popular social media websites include Facebook, Twitter, and LinkedIn.
5. If newly established businesses keep their networks and mind open, they can grow their networks tremendously.
6. It allows you to share the insights of your business with your customer on a one-to-one basis, giving them information about your products and services just the way they like and asking for their feedback directly for further improvement.

Syndicate the Content in Your Business to Online Website

1. Blog platforms and social networks are relatively a cheaper medium of effective advertisement and therefore must be exploited by all small businesses to gain maximum benefits. However, there are certain commitments you need to make if you really want your online marketing techniques to work.
   a. To keep up with an active presence on social media and to create online content for blogging, you need to dedicate at least 8-12 hours a week.
   b. Syndication is the only way you can effectively communicate with your customers and prospects online through providing relevant and fresh information and then spread that information across all the social networks you are using to share it with all your customers.
2. Syndicating online content helps you to spread information and/or message across the worldwide web.

So use it!

Expand Your Network

Expand your network by bonding with other entrepreneurs, especially ones with more experience. Social meetings with entrepreneurs give you an opportunity to learn about the market trends and gain more contacts.

Most importantly, you learn how experienced and skillful entrepreneurs think. You get a chance to learn from their mistakes, get to know about the opportunities in the market, and even pick their attitudes. This greatly works in your favor.

Home Work Time – The Best and Most Effective Business Plans

Setting up a business plan or establishing a business both requires proper homework. While it is always encouraged that you do what you love doing when you get a chance to become an entrepreneur, this might not always work in your favor. In short, you need to learn about the market, the changing trends, the requirements and demands of customers, and even about the most successful businesses, products, and services to start off well.

You may want to do something exceptional in the designing industry, but with the level of growing competition and cost, this may not be a suitable idea for you. Thus, homework is important to learn whether you should go ahead with the business plan you have in your mind or not.

Do your research on which businesses are doing best in a particular year and what type of businesses can be a success in that year. This will help you come up with several plans and options. Now conduct and evaluate each business according to each section mentioned above and find out which business will really make you a successful entrepreneur.

The following steps will help you decide:

1. Follow your passion: When you have a list in your hand, the best option will be to get in a business that you are interested in and that you would love to do. Of course, there are many advantages of following your passion.

2. Stay real: It is crucial to keep your expertise and individual interest in mind when starting a business. This is important because this way you will be sure your business represents a concrete entrepreneurial opportunity.
3. Keep competition in mind: Do your homework and survey the market to identify the level of established competition. Open your eyes wider here. You really need to see if someone has already established your idea and beaten you to the business. If this is the case, you need to see your other business options.

Now put all your options in a list, evaluate each one of them in detail, and decide accordingly for the best business you would like to undertake.

The best and most effective business plan for you is just a step away now!

Final Word

Many different types of people are attracted to the idea of becoming their own boss and becoming entrepreneurs. A variety of personal traits, aptitudes, and talents help to contribute towards an entrepreneurial vision, personality, and spirit. The character, passion, mindset, and attitude that define a successful entrepreneur can sometimes become difficult to identify, pinpoint, or sum up in one profile. However, it is easy to recognize if you have an entrepreneur within.

Evaluate and examine yourself for some of the most predominant characteristics of a true entrepreneur. Once you identify them, you will be able to nurture them, emulate, and develop them with time. You will also be able to acknowledge whether or not you really have what it takes to become a leader. It's the best way to evaluate whether you are suited for an entrepreneurial career. Of course, not everyone can be an entrepreneur – or a successful entrepreneur to put it right – and it is important to understand and accept that fact. If not taken seriously, you may risk money, effort, time, and energy trying to setup your own business only to discover later that it is not something destined for you.

If you believe you are perfectly suitable for an entrepreneurial career – and if it represents the achievement of your desire, potential, financial and personal dreams – understanding and learning how to list, verbalize, and define the fundamentals or temperament of a successful entrepreneur can tremendously help you.

Studying the traits and symptoms of a successful entrepreneur before you begin can grant you added fuel and hope. Having a checklist or inventory of specific qualities you can refer to as principles or guidelines can offer a path to better clarify your sense of purpose. Also, it will help you achieve objectives, which will further take you towards bigger benchmarks and achievement of higher goals. And grasping in a tangible and practical way the successful leader/entrepreneur disposition can give you a tremendously inspiring foresight, self-confidence, and determination when you realize that you, too, possess that absolutely amazing, winning attitude.

This book has all the details that will take you closer to the goal of becoming your own boss. Use the information shared in this book for your benefit and become a success story and inspiration for all the new entrepreneurs.

Good luck!